WASHOE COUNTY LIBRARY

3 1235 03597 8050

P9-CJS-259

EXPLORING BEYOND OUR SOLAR SYSTEM

BY PATRICIA HUTCHISON

Published by The Child's World®
1980 Lookout Drive • Mankato, MN 56003-1705
800-599-READ • www.childsworld.com

Acknowledgments
The Child's World®: Mary Berendes, Publishing Director
Red Line Editorial: Design, editorial direction, and production
Photographs ©: NASA/AP Images, cover, 1; NASA, 4; STScI/NASA, 7, 9, 10, 15; NASA,
ESA, HEIC, and The Hubble Heritage Team, 13, 23; Ben Cooper/SuperStock/Corbis,
16; NASA/Ames/JPL-Caltech, 19; NASA Ames/JPL-Caltech/T. Pyle, 20

Copyright © 2016 by The Child's World®
All rights reserved. No part of this book may be reproduced or utilized in any form or
by any means without written permission from the publisher.

ISBN 9781634074759

LCCN 2015946224

Printed in the United States of America
Mankato, MN
December, 2015
PA02280

ABOUT THE AUTHOR

Patricia Hutchison started her writing career while developing materials
for her own special education classroom. She first published science
materials for an educational website. Nonfiction, especially science, is her
passion because there are so many topics to explore. She gets much of her
inspiration from nature while she travels with her husband.

TABLE OF
CONTENTS

Chapter 1
HUBBLE PEERS INTO SPACE 5

Chapter 2
**HUBBLE EXPLORES
THE UNIVERSE** 11

Chapter 3
KEPLER, THE PLANET HUNTER 17

Glossary 22
Source Notes 23
To Learn More 24
Index 24

HUBBLE PEERS INTO SPACE

In 1609, Galileo gazed through his telescope into the night sky. He saw things no one had seen before. Mountains on the moon and distant stars appeared before his eyes. Since that time, **astronomers** have dreamed of seeing farther and deeper into space. Three **centuries** later, the Hubble Space Telescope made that dream come true.

On April 24, 1990, Hubble blasted into space. It was tucked inside the space shuttle *Discovery*. Hubble took its place 343 miles (552 km) above Earth's surface.

Scientists had been dreaming of a space telescope for years. They were frustrated by the telescopes on Earth. The planet's atmosphere has pockets of air that twist the light coming through it. This changes the way we see stars and other objects in space. But Hubble's perch above the atmosphere gives us a clear view.

◄ *Discovery* **blasts off with the Hubble Space Telescope aboard.**

One scientist said, "The reason we have the stars twinkle at night is because the light is being . . . blurred by the atmosphere around the Earth. That is why the Hubble Space Telescope is so good, because it is above the atmosphere."[1]

Hubble is about the size of a large school bus. It whirls around Earth at 18,000 miles per hour (29,000 km/h). Like telescopes on the ground, Hubble gathers light with its huge mirrors. Once the light is captured, the telescope's instruments work together to see objects deep in space.

Back in 1990, scientists anxiously waited for the first pictures from Hubble. But when they saw the photos, their hearts sank. The pictures were blurry! The telescope's biggest mirror was the wrong shape. Engineers worked to solve the problem. Finally, after three years, they had a solution.

On December 2, 1993, the space shuttle *Endeavour* blasted off from Earth. A crew of engineers rushed to the ailing telescope. Walking in space for five days, they completely rebuilt Hubble. It was one of the most difficult space missions ever.

Hubble was ready to try again in January 1994. Astronomers saw a beautiful image. Sparkling stars glowed throughout clouds

The Hubble Space Telescope gave astronomers ▶ a clear view of galaxy M100.

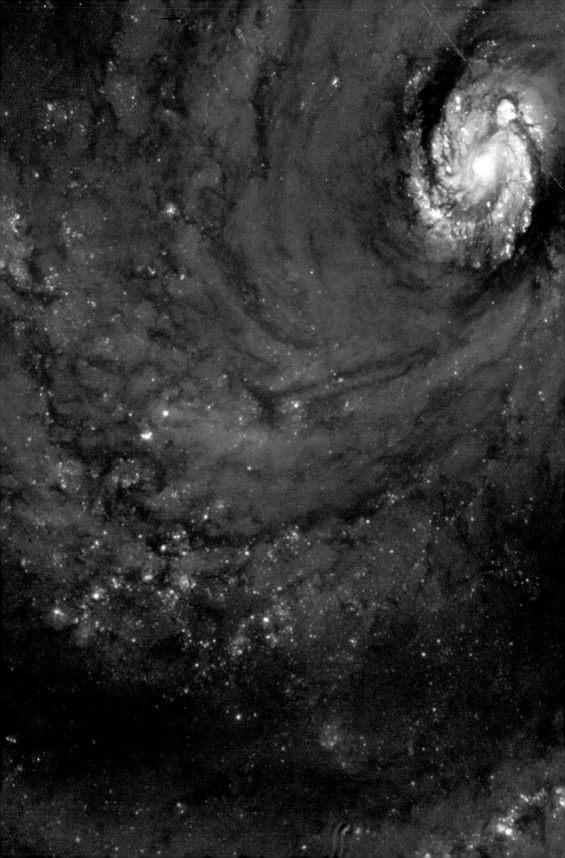

of gleaming dust. Together, they whirled around a blazing bright center. This was **galaxy** M100, millions of **light-years** away.

Astronomers soon put Hubble to a test. They turned it on an empty patch of sky. It soaked up all the light it could for ten days. This was a risk. The time could have all been wasted. Perhaps Hubble would see nothing at all. But that was not the case.

Astronomers were amazed as they observed a **cosmic** carnival of lights. More than 3,000 galaxies were glowing deep in space. They were all shapes and sizes. Scientists saw fireworks of red, green, and yellow. This image was called Hubble Deep Field.

Scientists knew they could not travel back in time. But thanks to Hubble, they could look back in time. How could they do this? Stars in the galaxies give off light. Light always travels at the same speed. So, if a star is far away, it takes a long time for its light to reach Hubble's mirrors. By the time it does, the telescope is looking at something that happened long ago.

This fact helped scientists make an important discovery. Before Hubble, scientists were trying to guess the age of the universe. Hubble helped to narrow it down. Scientists estimated that the universe is 13.7 billion years old. When scientists look through Hubble into deep space, they see objects the way they were when the universe was young.

▲ Every bright dot in the Hubble Deep Field is a galaxy containing billions of stars.

Chapter 2

HUBBLE EXPLORES THE UNIVERSE

Hubble showed astronomers that the universe was very different long ago. They saw galaxies that were smaller than the ones we see today. These galaxies were like bumper cars, constantly crashing into each other. They grew over millions of years. Today, they are huge **spirals** and ovals, filled with billions of stars. Scientists measured these giants and found that they are thousands of light-years across.

Astronomers used Hubble to see deeper into these galaxies. They made another surprising discovery. Gas was swirling around the center of galaxy M87. At the center of M87 was a massive black hole. Black holes are hungry monsters of gravity. They suck up anything that comes near them. Black holes are not empty space. They are actually a great amount of matter packed into a

◀ **A huge jet of particles shoots out of the center of galaxy M87.**

flow out from it, like ripples in a pond. Scientists have studied hundreds of pictures of nebulas. They have discovered that nebulas are like snowflakes. No two are exactly alike.

Astronomers were excited to discover that a larger star dies in a different way. The star's core heats up over time. Finally, it bursts from the center of the star. Matter is pushed away in a blinding flash of light and color. These giant fireworks are called supernovas.

Soon after Hubble was launched, it showed astronomers Supernova 1987A. They saw glowing red rings surrounding the exploding star in the center. Scientists had known about this supernova for several years. But other telescopes did not give scientists such clear images. "The sharp pictures from the Hubble telescope help us ask and answer new questions about Supernova 1987A," said one scientist. "In fact, without Hubble we wouldn't even know what to ask."[2]

Engineers have worked hard to repair and improve Hubble over the years. Sadly, its time will end one day. Hubble will slowly stop working. But scientists are amazed at the many fantastic discoveries it has made. They know that the images it has taken of the universe will live on.

A photo from the Hubble Space Telescope shows ▶ Supernova 1987A in amazing detail.

Chapter 3

KEPLER, THE PLANET HUNTER

Scientists had an important question. If there are other stars like our Sun, are there other planets around these stars? NASA began a mission to find out.

In 2009, a Delta II rocket blasted off from its launch pad. The rocket was carrying NASA's Kepler Space Telescope. Once the telescope was in space, astronomers started keeping watch on a small patch of the sky. That patch contains about 150,000 stars like our Sun. Scientists hoped some of these stars had **exoplanets**.

Through Kepler, astronomers watched the same stars all the time. Instruments in the telescope measured light. Scientists could notice a slight dimming of a star's brightness. This dimming is called a transit. It happens when a planet passes in front of the star. If the star dims again, scientists note the amount of time since the first dimming. They wait to see if it happens again in the

◀ **A scientist works on the Kepler Space Telescope before it is launched into space.**

same amount of time. When it does, they know they have found a planet.

Only three days after they began looking through Kepler, astronomers were excited to see a distant star dim. They continued to observe it, using the transit method. Looking through Kepler, astronomers were thrilled to see the third transit in December 2010. They had found the first exoplanet!

Scientists named the planet Kepler-22b. It is 600 light-years away. Since this first exciting discovery, scientists have found many other exoplanets. Some are rocky, like Earth. Others are completely covered with water.

In February 2014, scientists studied the data from the planet hunter. They announced that Kepler had found 715 new worlds. So far this was the largest number **confirmed** at one time. Through Kepler, astronomers also have noticed more than 150 stars that have more than one planet orbiting them.

In 2015, scientists announced the discovery of a planet called Kepler-452b. This planet is about the same size as Earth. And it orbits its star at about the same distance as Earth orbits the Sun. The scientists said it was possible that Kepler-452b had liquid water. With water, life would be possible. "Today, Earth is a little less lonely," said one scientist.[3]

An artist's concept of Kepler-22b ▶

▲ Kepler-452b, seen in this artist's concept, orbits its star every 385 days.

As of 2015, scientists had found more than 4,600 possible planets. They confirmed that more than 1,000 of these are true exoplanets. By measuring the temperatures on their surfaces, scientists believe conditions are just right for supporting liquid water. **Organisms** could survive on these planets.

Scientists wonder what they might find next. They have already found exoplanets much like Earth. This discovery allows scientists to focus on another question. Could there be life on any exoplanets?

DISTANCES IN SPACE

Object	Distance from Earth
Sun	0.000015 light-years
Proxima Centauri (closest star to the Sun)	4.2 light-years
Sirius (brightest star in the sky)	8.6 light-years
Center of the Milky Way galaxy	30,000 light-years
Andromeda (nearest large galaxy)	2.3 million light-years

GLOSSARY

astronomers (uh-STRON-uh-murz): Astronomers are scientists who study the stars and other objects in space. Astronomers have found more than 1,000 new planets.

centuries (SEN-chur-eez): Centuries are periods of one hundred years. Hubble was launched three centuries after Galileo used his homemade telescope.

confirmed (kuhn-FURMD): Confirmed means proved to be true. Scientists have confirmed more than 1,000 exoplanets in the universe so far.

cosmic (KOZ-mik): Cosmic means having to do with the universe. Hubble saw a cosmic carnival of lights.

exoplanets (EKS-oh-plan-uhts): Exoplanets are planets that are found beyond our solar system. Kepler has found thousands of possible exoplanets.

galaxy (GAL-uhks-ee): A galaxy is a collection of billions of stars. Hubble studied our galaxy, the Milky Way.

light-years (LYT-yeerz): Light-years are units of length; they are the distance light can travel in one year. Giant galaxies can be thousands of light-years across.

organisms (OR-guhn-iz-uhmz): Organisms are living things. Astronomers have found other planets where organisms could survive.

spirals (SPY-ruhlz): Spirals wind around a center and gradually get closer to or farther away from it. Some galaxies are huge spirals, while other galaxies are shaped like ovals.

SOURCE NOTES

1. Alejandro Rojas. "NASA Astronaut Discusses *Gravity* and the Dangers of Spacewalking." *Huffington Post*. TheHuffingtonPost.com, Inc., 3 Oct. 2013. Web. 12 Aug. 2015.

2. "NASA's Hubble Telescope Celebrates SN 1987A's 20th Anniversary." *HubbleSite*. Space Telescope Science Institute, 22 Feb. 2007. Web. 12 Aug. 2015.

3. Michael Pearson. "NASA finds 'Earth's bigger, older cousin.'" *CNN*. Turner Broadcasting System, 24 Jul. 2015. Web. 12 Aug. 2015.

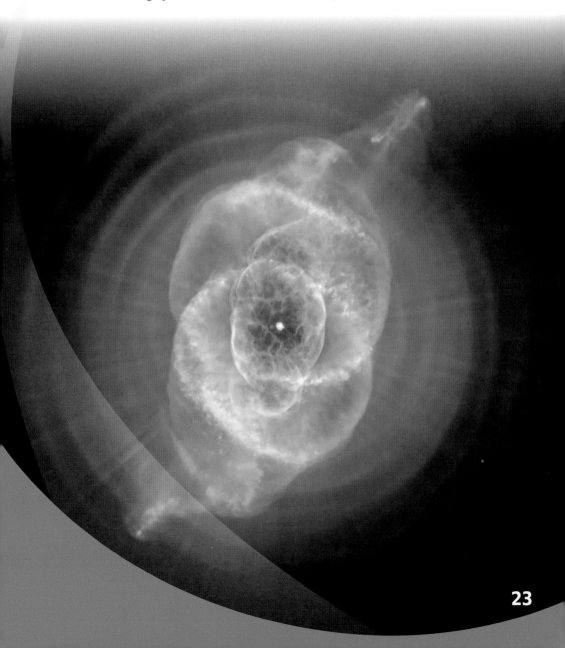

TO LEARN MORE

Books

Aguilar, David A., Christine Pulliam, and Patricia Daniels. *Space Encyclopedia: A Tour of Our Solar System and Beyond*. Washington, DC: National Geographic, 2013.

Space: A Visual Encyclopedia. New York: DK, 2010.

Wagner, Kathi, and Sheryl Racine. *The Everything Kids' Astronomy Book: Blast into Outer Space with Stellar Facts, Intergalactic Trivia, and Out-of-This-World Puzzles*. Avon, MA: Adams Media, 2008.

Web Sites

Visit our Web site for links about exploring beyond our solar system: childsworld.com/links

Note to Parents, Teachers, and Librarians: We routinely verify our Web links to make sure they are safe and active sites. So encourage your readers to check them out!

INDEX

black hole, 11–12

Cat's Eye Nebula, 12

Discovery, 5

Endeavour, 6

exoplanets, 17–18, 20–21

Galileo, 5

Hubble Deep Field, 8

Hubble Space Telescope, 5–6, 8, 11–12, 14

Kepler-22b, 18

Kepler-452b, 18

Kepler Space Telescope, 17–18

M87, 11

NASA, 17

Supernova 1987A, 14